45 Lime Recipes for Home

By: Kelly Johnson

Table of Contents

Appetizers and Snacks:

- Lime Cilantro Hummus
- Lime and Chili Roasted Nuts
- Lime Avocado Salsa
- Lime Garlic Edamame
- Lime Infused Guacamole

Salads:

- Grilled Chicken Lime Salad
- Shrimp and Mango Lime Salad
- Quinoa Lime Salad
- Watermelon and Feta Lime Salad
- Avocado Lime Caesar Salad

Main Courses:

- Cilantro Lime Chicken
- Tequila Lime Shrimp
- Lime and Honey Glazed Salmon
- Chili Lime Grilled Tofu
- Lime Chipotle Carnitas
- Coconut Lime Chicken Curry
- Lime Cilantro Beef Stir-Fry
- Baked Lime Tilapia

Sides:

- Lime Butter Asparagus
- Garlic Lime Roasted Brussels Sprouts
- Cilantro Lime Rice
- Lime Infused Quinoa
- Lime and Coconut Sweet Potato Mash

Soups:

- Lime Chicken Tortilla Soup
- Spicy Lime and Black Bean Soup
- Thai Coconut Lime Soup
- Avocado Lime Gazpacho

Beverages:

- Classic Lime Margarita
- Sparkling Cucumber Limeade
- Minty Lime Mojito
- Ginger Lime Iced Tea
- Watermelon Lime Slush

Desserts:

- Key Lime Pie
- Coconut Lime Bars
- Lime Sorbet
- Lime Cheesecake
- Margarita Cupcakes
- Lime and Coconut Panna Cotta
- Lime Posset
- Mango Lime Sorbet

Baked Goods:

- Lime Poppy Seed Muffins
- Coconut Lime Drizzle Cake
- Lime Zest Shortbread Cookies
- Blueberry Lime Scones
- Lime and Pistachio Biscotti

Appetizers and Snacks:

Lime Cilantro Hummus

Ingredients:

- 1 can (15 ounces) chickpeas, drained and rinsed
- 1/4 cup fresh cilantro leaves, packed
- 1/4 cup tahini
- 2 cloves garlic, minced
- Zest and juice of 2 limes
- 1/4 cup extra-virgin olive oil
- 1/2 teaspoon ground cumin
- Salt and black pepper, to taste
- Water (as needed for desired consistency)

Instructions:

Prepare Chickpeas:
- Rinse and drain the canned chickpeas thoroughly.

Combine Ingredients:
- In a food processor, combine chickpeas, fresh cilantro leaves, tahini, minced garlic, lime zest, lime juice, olive oil, ground cumin, salt, and black pepper.

Blend:
- Blend the ingredients until a coarse mixture forms.

Scrape Down Sides:
- Stop the food processor and scrape down the sides to ensure all ingredients are well incorporated.

Continue Blending:
- Continue blending while gradually adding water, one tablespoon at a time, until the hummus reaches your desired creamy consistency.

Taste and Adjust:
- Taste the Lime Cilantro Hummus and adjust the lime, salt, or other ingredients as needed to suit your preferences.

Serve:
- Transfer the hummus to a serving bowl. Drizzle with a bit of extra olive oil and garnish with additional cilantro leaves.

Enjoy:
- Serve the Lime Cilantro Hummus with pita bread, tortilla chips, vegetable sticks, or as a flavorful spread.

This Lime Cilantro Hummus is a refreshing twist on the classic hummus, with the citrusy zing of lime and the bright herbaceous flavor of cilantro. It's a perfect dip or spread for your snacks, appetizers, or as a tasty addition to your meals.

Lime and Chili Roasted Nuts

Ingredients:

- 2 cups mixed nuts (almonds, cashews, walnuts, pecans, etc.)
- 1 tablespoon olive oil
- Zest of 2 limes
- Juice of 1 lime
- 1 teaspoon chili powder
- 1/2 teaspoon cayenne pepper (adjust to taste)
- 1 teaspoon ground cumin
- 1 teaspoon paprika
- 1 tablespoon honey (optional, for a touch of sweetness)
- Salt, to taste

Instructions:

Preheat Oven:
- Preheat your oven to 350°F (175°C).

Prepare Nuts:
- In a large bowl, combine the mixed nuts.

Make Lime and Chili Coating:
- In a separate bowl, whisk together olive oil, lime zest, lime juice, chili powder, cayenne pepper, ground cumin, paprika, and honey (if using).

Coat Nuts:
- Pour the lime and chili mixture over the nuts, tossing to coat them evenly.

Spread on Baking Sheet:
- Spread the coated nuts in a single layer on a parchment-lined baking sheet.

Roast in the Oven:
- Roast the nuts in the preheated oven for 12-15 minutes, stirring halfway through, until they are golden brown and fragrant.

Cool:
- Allow the roasted nuts to cool completely on the baking sheet.

Season with Salt:
- Sprinkle the cooled nuts with salt to taste, tossing them to ensure even seasoning.

Serve:
- Serve the Lime and Chili Roasted Nuts as a snack or appetizer.

Store:
- Store any leftovers in an airtight container to maintain freshness.

Enjoy:
- Enjoy these zesty and spicy Lime and Chili Roasted Nuts as a flavorful and satisfying snack.

These Lime and Chili Roasted Nuts are a perfect combination of zesty citrus, heat from chili, and a variety of spices. They make a great party snack or a tasty topping for salads. Adjust the level of cayenne pepper based on your preference for spiciness.

Lime Avocado Salsa

Ingredients:

- 2 ripe avocados, diced
- 1 cup cherry tomatoes, halved
- 1/4 cup red onion, finely chopped
- 1 jalapeño, seeds removed and finely chopped
- 1/4 cup fresh cilantro, chopped
- Juice of 2 limes
- Salt and black pepper, to taste
- Optional: 1 clove garlic, minced

Instructions:

Prepare Ingredients:
- Dice the ripe avocados, halve the cherry tomatoes, finely chop the red onion, jalapeño, and cilantro.

Combine Ingredients:
- In a bowl, gently combine the diced avocados, halved cherry tomatoes, chopped red onion, chopped jalapeño, and chopped cilantro.

Add Lime Juice:
- Squeeze the juice of two limes over the avocado mixture. If you like it tangier, you can add more lime juice.

Season:
- Season the Lime Avocado Salsa with salt and black pepper to taste. If desired, add minced garlic for an extra layer of flavor.

Gently Toss:
- Gently toss all the ingredients together, making sure not to mash the avocados too much.

Chill (Optional):
- For enhanced flavors, you can refrigerate the salsa for about 30 minutes to allow the ingredients to meld.

Serve:
- Serve the Lime Avocado Salsa as a refreshing and vibrant topping for tacos, grilled chicken, fish, or as a dip with tortilla chips.

Enjoy:
- Enjoy the bright and zesty flavors of this Lime Avocado Salsa as a delicious addition to your favorite dishes or as a standalone appetizer.

This Lime Avocado Salsa is a quick and flavorful recipe that adds a burst of freshness to your meals. The combination of creamy avocados, juicy tomatoes, and zesty lime creates a versatile salsa that pairs well with various dishes. Adjust the spice level by modifying the amount of jalapeño used.

Lime Garlic Edamame

Ingredients:

- 2 cups edamame (fresh or frozen)
- 2 tablespoons olive oil
- 3 cloves garlic, minced
- Zest of 1 lime
- Juice of 1 lime
- Salt, to taste
- Black pepper, to taste
- Optional: Red pepper flakes for added heat
- Fresh cilantro or parsley, chopped (for garnish)

Instructions:

Prepare Edamame:
- If using frozen edamame, cook them according to the package instructions. If using fresh edamame, steam them until tender, about 5-7 minutes.

Make Lime Garlic Mixture:
- In a small bowl, mix together the olive oil, minced garlic, lime zest, and lime juice.

Sauté Garlic:
- In a large skillet or pan, heat the lime-garlic mixture over medium heat. Sauté the minced garlic for 1-2 minutes until it becomes fragrant.

Add Edamame:
- Add the cooked edamame to the skillet, tossing to coat them evenly with the lime and garlic mixture.

Season:
- Season the Lime Garlic Edamame with salt and black pepper to taste. If you like it spicy, you can also add red pepper flakes at this point.

Sauté:
- Sauté the edamame in the lime and garlic mixture for an additional 2-3 minutes, allowing the flavors to meld and the edamame to absorb the seasonings.

Garnish:
- Garnish the Lime Garlic Edamame with chopped fresh cilantro or parsley.

Serve:

- Serve the Lime Garlic Edamame as a flavorful and nutritious snack, side dish, or appetizer.

Enjoy:

- Enjoy the zesty and garlicky goodness of these Lime Garlic Edamame with a squeeze of lime for an extra burst of flavor.

This Lime Garlic Edamame is a simple and delicious way to enjoy the nutty flavor of edamame with a zesty and aromatic twist. It makes for a delightful appetizer or a healthy snack with a burst of citrusy freshness.

Lime Infused Guacamole

Ingredients:

- 3 ripe avocados
- 1 medium tomato, diced
- 1/4 cup red onion, finely chopped
- 1 jalapeño, seeds removed and finely chopped
- 1/4 cup fresh cilantro, chopped
- Juice of 2 limes
- Zest of 1 lime
- 1 clove garlic, minced
- Salt and black pepper, to taste

Instructions:

Prepare Avocados:
- Cut the avocados in half, remove the pits, and scoop the flesh into a mixing bowl.

Mash Avocados:
- Use a fork or potato masher to mash the avocados to your desired consistency. Some people prefer chunky guacamole, while others like it smoother.

Add Vegetables:
- Add the diced tomato, finely chopped red onion, chopped jalapeño, and minced garlic to the mashed avocados.

Add Lime Juice and Zest:
- Squeeze the juice of two limes into the bowl. Add the lime zest as well for an extra burst of citrus flavor.

Season:
- Season the Lime-Infused Guacamole with salt and black pepper to taste. Adjust the seasoning according to your preference.

Mix Well:
- Gently mix all the ingredients together, ensuring that the lime juice and zest are evenly distributed.

Add Cilantro:
- Fold in the chopped cilantro, distributing it throughout the guacamole.

Adjust Consistency:

- If needed, adjust the consistency by adding more lime juice or mashing the avocados further.

Chill (Optional):
- For enhanced flavors, you can refrigerate the guacamole for about 30 minutes to allow the ingredients to meld.

Serve:
- Serve the Lime-Infused Guacamole with tortilla chips, tacos, nachos, or as a side to your favorite Mexican dishes.

Enjoy:
- Enjoy the zesty and refreshing taste of this Lime-Infused Guacamole as a delicious dip or accompaniment to your meals.

This Lime-Infused Guacamole adds a vibrant and citrusy twist to the classic recipe, making it a perfect appetizer or condiment for various dishes. The lime zest and juice enhance the freshness of the guacamole, creating a delightful burst of flavor with every bite.

Salads:

Grilled Chicken Lime Salad

Ingredients:

For the Grilled Chicken:

- 4 boneless, skinless chicken breasts
- 2 tablespoons olive oil
- Zest of 2 limes
- Juice of 2 limes
- 2 cloves garlic, minced
- 1 teaspoon cumin
- Salt and black pepper, to taste

For the Salad:

- Mixed salad greens (lettuce, spinach, arugula, etc.)
- 1 cup cherry tomatoes, halved
- 1 cucumber, sliced
- 1 avocado, sliced
- 1/4 cup red onion, thinly sliced
- 1/4 cup feta cheese, crumbled (optional)

For the Lime Vinaigrette:

- 1/4 cup olive oil
- Zest of 1 lime
- Juice of 1 lime
- 1 tablespoon honey
- 1 teaspoon Dijon mustard
- Salt and black pepper, to taste

Instructions:

Prepare Chicken Marinade:

- In a bowl, whisk together olive oil, lime zest, lime juice, minced garlic, cumin, salt, and black pepper to create the marinade.

Marinate Chicken:
- Place the chicken breasts in a zip-top bag or shallow dish. Pour half of the marinade over the chicken, ensuring each piece is well-coated. Marinate in the refrigerator for at least 30 minutes, or longer for more flavor.

Preheat Grill:
- Preheat your grill to medium-high heat.

Grill Chicken:
- Remove the chicken from the marinade and discard the used marinade. Grill the chicken for about 6-8 minutes per side or until fully cooked, with an internal temperature of 165°F (74°C). Cooking time may vary depending on the thickness of the chicken breasts.

Rest and Slice:
- Allow the grilled chicken to rest for a few minutes before slicing it into strips.

Prepare Salad:
- In a large salad bowl, combine the mixed salad greens, cherry tomatoes, cucumber slices, avocado slices, red onion, and crumbled feta cheese (if using).

Make Lime Vinaigrette:
- In a small bowl, whisk together olive oil, lime zest, lime juice, honey, Dijon mustard, salt, and black pepper to create the vinaigrette.

Assemble Salad:
- Drizzle the lime vinaigrette over the salad and toss gently to combine.

Add Grilled Chicken:
- Arrange the sliced grilled chicken on top of the salad.

Serve:
- Serve the Grilled Chicken Lime Salad immediately, with extra lime wedges on the side.

Enjoy:
- Enjoy this refreshing and flavorful Grilled Chicken Lime Salad as a light and satisfying meal.

This Grilled Chicken Lime Salad is a delicious and healthy option that combines the charred flavor of grilled chicken with the freshness of lime-infused salad greens. The lime vinaigrette adds a zesty kick to the overall dish. It's perfect for a light lunch or dinner.

Shrimp and Mango Lime Salad

Ingredients:

For the Salad:

- 1 pound large shrimp, peeled and deveined
- 2 ripe mangoes, peeled, pitted, and diced
- 1 cucumber, diced
- 1 red bell pepper, diced
- 1/4 cup red onion, finely chopped
- 1/4 cup fresh cilantro, chopped
- Mixed salad greens (lettuce, spinach, arugula, etc.)

For the Lime Dressing:

- Juice of 2 limes
- Zest of 1 lime
- 3 tablespoons olive oil
- 1 tablespoon honey
- 1 teaspoon Dijon mustard
- Salt and black pepper, to taste

Instructions:

Prepare Shrimp:
- Season the peeled and deveined shrimp with salt and black pepper. Grill the shrimp until cooked through, about 2-3 minutes per side. Set aside to cool.

Prepare Salad Ingredients:
- In a large salad bowl, combine the diced mangoes, cucumber, red bell pepper, red onion, and fresh cilantro. Add the mixed salad greens.

Make Lime Dressing:
- In a small bowl, whisk together the lime juice, lime zest, olive oil, honey, Dijon mustard, salt, and black pepper. Adjust the sweetness and acidity to your taste.

Assemble Salad:

- Add the grilled shrimp to the salad ingredients in the bowl.

Drizzle with Dressing:
- Drizzle the lime dressing over the salad and toss gently to coat all the ingredients evenly.

Serve:
- Serve the Shrimp and Mango Lime Salad immediately, garnishing with extra cilantro if desired.

Enjoy:
- Enjoy this refreshing and flavorful Shrimp and Mango Lime Salad as a light and satisfying meal.

This Shrimp and Mango Lime Salad is a delightful combination of juicy shrimp, sweet mango, and crisp vegetables, all tossed in a zesty lime dressing. It's a perfect dish for a light lunch or dinner, and the vibrant flavors make it a refreshing choice for warm days.

Quinoa Lime Salad

Ingredients:

For the Salad:

- 1 cup quinoa, rinsed and cooked according to package instructions
- 1 cup cherry tomatoes, halved
- 1 cucumber, diced
- 1/2 red onion, finely chopped
- 1/4 cup fresh cilantro, chopped
- 1/4 cup feta cheese, crumbled (optional)
- Mixed salad greens (optional)

For the Lime Vinaigrette:

- Juice of 2 limes
- Zest of 1 lime
- 1/4 cup extra-virgin olive oil
- 1 clove garlic, minced
- 1 teaspoon honey or maple syrup
- Salt and black pepper, to taste

Instructions:

Prepare Quinoa:
- Rinse the quinoa under cold water and cook it according to the package instructions. Once cooked, let it cool to room temperature.

Make Lime Vinaigrette:
- In a small bowl, whisk together the lime juice, lime zest, olive oil, minced garlic, honey or maple syrup, salt, and black pepper. Adjust the sweetness and acidity to your taste.

Assemble Salad:
- In a large salad bowl, combine the cooked quinoa, cherry tomatoes, diced cucumber, chopped red onion, and fresh cilantro. If desired, add mixed salad greens for extra freshness.

Add Feta (Optional):
- If using feta cheese, crumble it over the salad.

Drizzle with Vinaigrette:

- Drizzle the lime vinaigrette over the salad and toss gently to coat all the ingredients evenly.

Chill (Optional):
- For enhanced flavors, refrigerate the Quinoa Lime Salad for about 30 minutes before serving.

Serve:
- Serve the Quinoa Lime Salad as a light and nutritious meal on its own or as a side dish.

Enjoy:
- Enjoy this vibrant and zesty Quinoa Lime Salad as a refreshing addition to your lunch or dinner.

This Quinoa Lime Salad is not only delicious but also packed with nutrients. The combination of quinoa, fresh vegetables, and the zesty lime vinaigrette creates a light and satisfying dish that can be enjoyed on its own or as a side. Customize it with your favorite ingredients to suit your taste.

Watermelon and Feta Lime Salad

Ingredients:

- 4 cups seedless watermelon, cubed
- 1 cup feta cheese, crumbled
- 1/4 cup fresh mint leaves, chopped
- Juice of 2 limes
- Zest of 1 lime
- 2 tablespoons extra-virgin olive oil
- 1 tablespoon honey
- Salt and black pepper, to taste

Instructions:

Prepare Watermelon:
- Cut the seedless watermelon into bite-sized cubes, removing any seeds.

Make Lime Dressing:
- In a small bowl, whisk together the lime juice, lime zest, extra-virgin olive oil, honey, salt, and black pepper to create the dressing.

Assemble Salad:
- In a large salad bowl, combine the cubed watermelon, crumbled feta cheese, and chopped fresh mint.

Drizzle with Dressing:
- Drizzle the lime dressing over the watermelon, feta, and mint. Gently toss to coat the ingredients evenly.

Chill (Optional):
- For enhanced flavors, refrigerate the Watermelon and Feta Lime Salad for about 15-30 minutes before serving.

Serve:
- Serve the salad in individual bowls or on a platter.

Garnish (Optional):
- Garnish with additional mint leaves for a fresh and vibrant presentation.

Enjoy:
- Enjoy the sweet and savory combination of watermelon and feta, elevated by the zesty lime dressing.

This Watermelon and Feta Lime Salad is a refreshing and delightful summer dish. The sweetness of the watermelon, the saltiness of the feta, and the citrusy kick from the lime dressing create a perfect harmony of flavors. It's an ideal side dish for barbecues, picnics, or any summer gathering.

Main Courses:

Cilantro Lime Chicken

Ingredients:

- 4 boneless, skinless chicken breasts
- 1/4 cup fresh cilantro, chopped
- Juice of 2 limes
- Zest of 1 lime
- 3 cloves garlic, minced
- 2 tablespoons olive oil
- 1 teaspoon ground cumin
- 1 teaspoon paprika
- Salt and black pepper, to taste

Instructions:

Prepare Marinade:
- In a bowl, combine chopped cilantro, lime juice, lime zest, minced garlic, olive oil, ground cumin, paprika, salt, and black pepper. Mix well to create the marinade.

Marinate Chicken:
- Place the chicken breasts in a resealable plastic bag or shallow dish. Pour the marinade over the chicken, ensuring it is well-coated. Seal the bag or cover the dish and refrigerate for at least 30 minutes to allow the flavors to meld.

Preheat Grill or Grill Pan:
- Preheat your grill or grill pan over medium-high heat.

Grill Chicken:
- Remove the chicken from the marinade and discard the marinade. Grill the chicken breasts for approximately 6-8 minutes per side or until the internal temperature reaches 165°F (74°C) and the chicken is cooked through.

Rest and Slice:
- Allow the grilled chicken to rest for a few minutes before slicing it into thin strips.

Serve:
- Serve the Cilantro Lime Chicken strips as a main course with your favorite side dishes, in tacos, or on top of a salad.

Garnish (Optional):
- Garnish with additional chopped cilantro and lime wedges for extra freshness.

Enjoy:
- Enjoy this Cilantro Lime Chicken for a flavorful and zesty meal that's perfect for summer grilling or anytime you want a burst of citrusy goodness.

This Cilantro Lime Chicken recipe offers a perfect blend of tangy lime and fresh cilantro, enhancing the natural flavors of the chicken. Whether grilled outdoors or cooked on a stovetop grill pan, it's a versatile dish that can be served in various ways to suit your preferences.

Tequila Lime Shrimp

Ingredients:

- 1 pound large shrimp, peeled and deveined
- 2 tablespoons tequila
- Zest and juice of 2 limes
- 3 cloves garlic, minced
- 2 tablespoons olive oil
- 1 teaspoon chili powder
- 1 teaspoon cumin
- Salt and black pepper, to taste
- Fresh cilantro, chopped (for garnish)
- Lime wedges (for serving)

Instructions:

Marinate Shrimp:
- In a bowl, combine tequila, lime zest, lime juice, minced garlic, olive oil, chili powder, cumin, salt, and black pepper. Mix well to create the marinade.

Add Shrimp to Marinade:
- Add the peeled and deveined shrimp to the marinade, ensuring they are well-coated. Allow the shrimp to marinate for at least 15-30 minutes to absorb the flavors.

Preheat Skillet or Grill Pan:
- Heat a skillet or grill pan over medium-high heat.

Cook Shrimp:
- Remove the shrimp from the marinade and place them in the hot skillet or grill pan. Cook for 2-3 minutes per side or until the shrimp turn pink and opaque.

Deglaze with Tequila (Optional):
- For an extra burst of tequila flavor, you can deglaze the pan with a splash of tequila after cooking the shrimp. Be cautious, as the alcohol may ignite briefly.

Garnish:
- Garnish the Tequila Lime Shrimp with chopped fresh cilantro.

Serve:
- Serve the shrimp hot with lime wedges on the side.

Enjoy:
- Enjoy these Tequila Lime Shrimp as an appetizer, taco filling, or as part of a delicious seafood dish.

This Tequila Lime Shrimp recipe infuses the shrimp with the bold flavors of tequila, lime, and aromatic spices. Whether cooked on a skillet or grill pan, these shrimp are quick to prepare and make a flavorful addition to various dishes.

Lime and Honey Glazed Salmon

Ingredients:

- 4 salmon fillets
- 3 tablespoons honey
- Zest and juice of 2 limes
- 2 tablespoons soy sauce
- 2 cloves garlic, minced
- 1 tablespoon olive oil
- Salt and black pepper, to taste
- Fresh cilantro, chopped (for garnish)

Instructions:

Preheat Oven:
- Preheat your oven to 400°F (200°C).

Prepare Glaze:
- In a bowl, whisk together honey, lime zest, lime juice, soy sauce, minced garlic, olive oil, salt, and black pepper to create the glaze.

Marinate Salmon:
- Place the salmon fillets in a shallow dish and brush them with half of the prepared glaze. Allow the salmon to marinate for 15-30 minutes.

Cook Salmon:
- Transfer the marinated salmon fillets to a baking sheet lined with parchment paper. Bake in the preheated oven for 12-15 minutes or until the salmon is cooked through and flakes easily with a fork.

Glaze Again:
- During the last few minutes of cooking, brush the salmon with the remaining glaze to create a shiny and flavorful coating.

Broil (Optional):
- If desired, you can broil the salmon for an additional 1-2 minutes at the end to caramelize the glaze slightly.

Garnish:
- Garnish the Lime and Honey Glazed Salmon with chopped fresh cilantro.

Serve:
- Serve the salmon hot with your favorite side dishes, such as rice, quinoa, or steamed vegetables.

Enjoy:

- Enjoy this delicious and easy-to-make Lime and Honey Glazed Salmon with a perfect balance of sweet and tangy flavors.

This Lime and Honey Glazed Salmon recipe creates a tasty and vibrant dish that's perfect for a quick and flavorful dinner. The combination of honey, lime, and soy sauce provides a delightful glaze that enhances the natural richness of the salmon.

Chili Lime Grilled Tofu

Ingredients:

- 1 block (14-16 ounces) extra-firm tofu, pressed and drained
- 2 tablespoons soy sauce or tamari (for a gluten-free option)
- Zest and juice of 2 limes
- 2 tablespoons olive oil
- 1 tablespoon chili powder
- 1 teaspoon cumin
- 1 teaspoon smoked paprika
- 1 teaspoon garlic powder
- 1 teaspoon onion powder
- Salt and black pepper, to taste
- Fresh cilantro, chopped (for garnish)
- Lime wedges (for serving)

Instructions:

Prepare Tofu:
- Press the tofu to remove excess water. Cut the pressed tofu into slices or cubes, depending on your preference.

Make Marinade:
- In a bowl, whisk together soy sauce (or tamari), lime zest, lime juice, olive oil, chili powder, cumin, smoked paprika, garlic powder, onion powder, salt, and black pepper to create the marinade.

Marinate Tofu:
- Place the tofu in a shallow dish and pour half of the marinade over it. Allow the tofu to marinate for at least 15-30 minutes.

Preheat Grill:
- Preheat your grill or grill pan over medium-high heat.

Grill Tofu:
- Grill the marinated tofu for about 4-5 minutes per side or until it develops grill marks and becomes golden brown.

Brush with Marinade:
- During grilling, brush the tofu with the remaining marinade to enhance the flavor.

Garnish:

- Garnish the Chili Lime Grilled Tofu with chopped fresh cilantro.

Serve:
- Serve the grilled tofu hot with lime wedges on the side.

Enjoy:
- Enjoy the Chili Lime Grilled Tofu as a flavorful and protein-rich main course or as a delicious addition to salads, tacos, or bowls.

This Chili Lime Grilled Tofu recipe offers a perfect combination of smoky, spicy, and citrusy flavors. It's a versatile dish that can be served on its own or incorporated into various meals. Adjust the spice level according to your taste preferences.

Lime Chipotle Carnitas

Ingredients:

For the Carnitas:

- 3-4 pounds pork shoulder, cut into chunks
- 2 tablespoons vegetable oil
- 1 onion, chopped
- 4 cloves garlic, minced
- 2 teaspoons ground cumin
- 2 teaspoons dried oregano
- Salt and black pepper, to taste
- 1 cup chicken broth
- Juice of 3 limes
- Zest of 1 lime

For the Lime Chipotle Sauce:

- 2 chipotle peppers in adobo sauce, minced
- 1/4 cup fresh cilantro, chopped
- Juice of 1 lime
- Zest of 1 lime
- Salt and black pepper, to taste

Instructions:

Season Pork:
- Season the pork chunks with salt, black pepper, ground cumin, and dried oregano.

Sear Pork:
- In a large Dutch oven or heavy-bottomed pot, heat vegetable oil over medium-high heat. Sear the pork chunks on all sides until browned. Work in batches if necessary. Remove pork from the pot and set aside.

Sauté Aromatics:
- In the same pot, sauté chopped onions until softened. Add minced garlic and sauté for an additional minute.

Deglaze Pot:
- Pour in the chicken broth to deglaze the pot, scraping up any browned bits from the bottom.

Return Pork to Pot:
- Return the seared pork chunks to the pot. Add lime juice and lime zest.

Simmer and Cook:
- Bring the mixture to a simmer, then cover the pot and reduce the heat. Allow the pork to cook on low heat for 2-3 hours or until it becomes tender and can be easily shredded with a fork.

Make Lime Chipotle Sauce:
- In a separate bowl, mix minced chipotle peppers, chopped cilantro, lime juice, lime zest, salt, and black pepper to create the Lime Chipotle Sauce.

Shred Pork:
- Once the pork is tender, use two forks to shred it in the pot. Allow the shredded pork to absorb the cooking juices.

Add Lime Chipotle Sauce:
- Pour the Lime Chipotle Sauce over the shredded pork and stir to combine. Simmer for an additional 15-20 minutes to allow the flavors to meld.

Adjust Seasoning:
- Taste and adjust the seasoning, adding more salt, pepper, or lime juice if needed.

Serve:
- Serve the Lime Chipotle Carnitas in tacos, burritos, bowls, or on its own. Garnish with additional cilantro and lime wedges if desired.

Enjoy:
- Enjoy the flavorful and zesty Lime Chipotle Carnitas as a delicious and versatile dish.

This Lime Chipotle Carnitas recipe combines tender and succulent pork with a zesty lime chipotle sauce, creating a dish that's perfect for tacos, burritos, bowls, or any Mexican-inspired meal. Adjust the spice level by modifying the amount of chipotle peppers.

Coconut Lime Chicken Curry

Ingredients:

- 1.5 lbs boneless, skinless chicken thighs, cut into bite-sized pieces
- 2 tablespoons vegetable oil
- 1 large onion, finely chopped
- 3 cloves garlic, minced
- 1 tablespoon ginger, grated
- 2 tablespoons red curry paste
- 1 can (14 oz) coconut milk
- 1 cup chicken broth
- Zest and juice of 2 limes
- 2 tablespoons fish sauce
- 1 tablespoon soy sauce
- 1 tablespoon brown sugar
- 1 red bell pepper, sliced
- 1 cup snow peas, trimmed
- Fresh cilantro, chopped (for garnish)
- Cooked jasmine rice (for serving)

Instructions:

Sear Chicken:
- In a large skillet or wok, heat the vegetable oil over medium-high heat. Add the chicken pieces and sear until browned on all sides. Remove chicken from the skillet and set aside.

Sauté Aromatics:
- In the same skillet, add chopped onions and sauté until softened. Add minced garlic and grated ginger, sautéing for an additional minute.

Add Curry Paste:
- Stir in the red curry paste and cook for 1-2 minutes to release its flavors.

Pour Coconut Milk:
- Pour in the coconut milk, chicken broth, lime zest, lime juice, fish sauce, soy sauce, and brown sugar. Stir to combine.

Simmer Curry:

- Return the seared chicken to the skillet. Bring the mixture to a simmer, cover, and let it cook on low heat for about 20-25 minutes or until the chicken is cooked through and tender.

Add Vegetables:
- Add sliced red bell pepper and trimmed snow peas to the curry. Simmer for an additional 5-7 minutes until the vegetables are crisp-tender.

Adjust Seasoning:
- Taste the curry and adjust the seasoning if needed, adding more fish sauce, soy sauce, or lime juice according to your preference.

Serve:
- Serve the Coconut Lime Chicken Curry over cooked jasmine rice.

Garnish:
- Garnish with chopped fresh cilantro.

Enjoy:
- Enjoy this Coconut Lime Chicken Curry for a flavorful and aromatic Thai-inspired meal.

This Coconut Lime Chicken Curry is a delightful combination of creamy coconut, zesty lime, and aromatic spices. It's a comforting and flavorful dish that pairs well with jasmine rice. Adjust the level of spiciness by modifying the amount of red curry paste.

Lime Cilantro Beef Stir-Fry

Ingredients:

For the Beef Marinade:

- 1 pound flank steak, thinly sliced against the grain
- 2 tablespoons soy sauce
- 1 tablespoon oyster sauce
- 1 tablespoon cornstarch
- 1 tablespoon sesame oil
- 1 teaspoon sugar
- 1 teaspoon black pepper

For the Stir-Fry:

- 2 tablespoons vegetable oil
- 3 cloves garlic, minced
- 1 tablespoon ginger, grated
- 1 red bell pepper, thinly sliced
- 1 yellow bell pepper, thinly sliced
- 1 cup snap peas, ends trimmed
- Zest and juice of 2 limes
- 2 tablespoons soy sauce
- 1 tablespoon fish sauce
- 1 tablespoon hoisin sauce
- 1 tablespoon chopped cilantro (for garnish)
- Cooked rice (for serving)

Instructions:

Marinate Beef:
- In a bowl, combine thinly sliced flank steak with soy sauce, oyster sauce, cornstarch, sesame oil, sugar, and black pepper. Allow the beef to marinate for at least 15-30 minutes.

Heat Wok or Skillet:
- Heat vegetable oil in a wok or large skillet over high heat.

Sear Beef:

- Add the marinated beef to the hot wok or skillet and sear for 2-3 minutes until browned. Remove the beef from the wok and set aside.

Sauté Aromatics:
- In the same wok, add minced garlic and grated ginger. Sauté for about 30 seconds until fragrant.

Add Vegetables:
- Add thinly sliced red and yellow bell peppers along with snap peas to the wok. Stir-fry for 2-3 minutes until the vegetables are crisp-tender.

Combine Beef and Vegetables:
- Return the seared beef to the wok and toss to combine with the vegetables.

Make Sauce:
- In a small bowl, mix lime zest, lime juice, soy sauce, fish sauce, and hoisin sauce to create the sauce.

Pour Sauce:
- Pour the sauce over the beef and vegetables. Toss to coat evenly and cook for an additional 1-2 minutes.

Garnish:
- Garnish the Lime Cilantro Beef Stir-Fry with chopped cilantro.

Serve:
- Serve the stir-fry over cooked rice.

Enjoy:
- Enjoy this zesty and flavorful Lime Cilantro Beef Stir-Fry as a quick and delicious meal.

This Lime Cilantro Beef Stir-Fry brings together tender marinated beef, vibrant vegetables, and a zesty lime-infused sauce. It's a perfect dish for a quick and satisfying weeknight dinner served over a bed of steamed rice. Adjust the level of spiciness by adding red pepper flakes if desired.

Baked Lime Tilapia

Ingredients:

- 4 tilapia fillets
- 2 tablespoons olive oil
- Zest and juice of 2 limes
- 2 cloves garlic, minced
- 1 teaspoon chili powder
- 1 teaspoon cumin
- Salt and black pepper, to taste
- Fresh cilantro, chopped (for garnish)
- Lime wedges (for serving)

Instructions:

Preheat Oven:
- Preheat your oven to 400°F (200°C).

Prepare Marinade:
- In a bowl, mix together olive oil, lime zest, lime juice, minced garlic, chili powder, cumin, salt, and black pepper to create the marinade.

Marinate Tilapia:
- Place the tilapia fillets in a baking dish. Pour the marinade over the tilapia, making sure each fillet is well-coated. Allow the fish to marinate for 15-30 minutes.

Bake Tilapia:
- Bake the tilapia in the preheated oven for 12-15 minutes or until the fish flakes easily with a fork and is opaque in the center.

Broil (Optional):
- If desired, you can broil the tilapia for an additional 1-2 minutes at the end to add a golden finish.

Garnish:
- Garnish the Baked Lime Tilapia with chopped fresh cilantro.

Serve:
- Serve the tilapia hot, either on its own or with your favorite side dishes.

Lime Wedges:
- Serve with lime wedges on the side for an extra burst of citrus.

Enjoy:

- Enjoy this Baked Lime Tilapia for a light and flavorful meal that's easy to prepare.

This Baked Lime Tilapia recipe combines the zesty flavors of lime with aromatic spices to create a delicious and healthy dish. The tilapia is marinated to infuse it with the citrusy and savory notes, resulting in a quick and flavorful baked fish. Serve it with rice, quinoa, or a side salad for a complete meal.

Sides:

Lime Butter Asparagus

Ingredients:

- 1 pound fresh asparagus, trimmed
- 2 tablespoons unsalted butter
- Zest and juice of 1 lime
- 2 cloves garlic, minced
- Salt and black pepper, to taste
- Crushed red pepper flakes (optional, for heat)
- Chopped fresh parsley (for garnish)

Instructions:

Blanch Asparagus:
- Bring a large pot of salted water to a boil. Add the trimmed asparagus and blanch for 2-3 minutes until they are bright green and slightly tender. Immediately transfer the asparagus to a bowl of ice water to stop the cooking process. Drain and set aside.

Prepare Lime Butter Sauce:
- In a small saucepan, melt the butter over medium heat. Add minced garlic and sauté for about 1 minute until fragrant.

Add Lime Zest and Juice:
- Stir in the lime zest and lime juice into the melted butter and garlic mixture. Cook for an additional 1-2 minutes, allowing the flavors to meld.

Season with Salt and Pepper:
- Season the lime butter sauce with salt and black pepper to taste. Add crushed red pepper flakes if you desire a bit of heat.

Saute Asparagus:
- In a large skillet, heat the lime butter sauce over medium-high heat. Add the blanched asparagus and sauté for 2-3 minutes, tossing to coat the asparagus evenly.

Garnish:
- Garnish the Lime Butter Asparagus with chopped fresh parsley for added freshness and color.

Serve:

- Serve the asparagus hot as a side dish.

Enjoy:
- Enjoy this simple and elegant Lime Butter Asparagus with the delightful combination of citrusy lime and rich butter.

This Lime Butter Asparagus recipe provides a burst of citrusy flavor that complements the natural sweetness of fresh asparagus. It's a quick and easy side dish that pairs well with various main courses, adding a touch of brightness to your meal. Adjust the seasoning and spice level according to your taste preferences.

Garlic Lime Roasted Brussels Sprouts

Ingredients:

- 1 pound Brussels sprouts, trimmed and halved
- 3 tablespoons olive oil
- 4 cloves garlic, minced
- Zest and juice of 1 lime
- 1 teaspoon honey or maple syrup (optional)
- Salt and black pepper, to taste
- Red pepper flakes (optional, for heat)
- Fresh parsley, chopped (for garnish)

Instructions:

Preheat Oven:
- Preheat your oven to 400°F (200°C).

Prepare Brussels Sprouts:
- Trim the Brussels sprouts and cut them in half. If they are large, you can quarter them for even cooking.

Make Garlic Lime Marinade:
- In a bowl, mix together olive oil, minced garlic, lime zest, lime juice, honey or maple syrup (if using), salt, black pepper, and red pepper flakes (if adding spice).

Coat Brussels Sprouts:
- Toss the Brussels sprouts in the garlic lime marinade until they are well-coated.

Roast in Oven:
- Spread the Brussels sprouts in a single layer on a baking sheet. Roast in the preheated oven for 20-25 minutes or until the edges are crispy and golden brown, tossing halfway through for even cooking.

Garnish:
- Remove the roasted Brussels sprouts from the oven and garnish with chopped fresh parsley for added color and freshness.

Serve:
- Serve the Garlic Lime Roasted Brussels Sprouts hot as a flavorful and nutritious side dish.

Enjoy:

- Enjoy these roasted Brussels sprouts with a delightful combination of garlic and lime that enhances their natural flavors.

This Garlic Lime Roasted Brussels Sprouts recipe adds a zesty and aromatic twist to the classic roasted Brussels sprouts. The combination of garlic and lime brings brightness to the dish, making it a delicious and healthy side that pairs well with a variety of main courses. Adjust the level of sweetness and spice according to your preferences.

Cilantro Lime Rice

Ingredients:

- 1 cup long-grain white rice
- 2 cups water
- 1 tablespoon unsalted butter or olive oil
- 1 teaspoon salt
- Zest and juice of 2 limes
- 1/4 cup fresh cilantro, finely chopped

Instructions:

Rinse Rice:
- Rinse the rice under cold water until the water runs clear. This helps remove excess starch.

Cook Rice:
- In a medium saucepan, combine the rinsed rice, water, butter or olive oil, and salt. Bring to a boil over high heat.

Simmer:
- Once boiling, reduce the heat to low, cover the saucepan, and simmer for 15-18 minutes or until the rice is tender and the water is absorbed.

Fluff Rice:
- Remove the saucepan from heat and let it sit, covered, for 5 minutes. Fluff the rice with a fork to separate the grains.

Add Lime Zest and Juice:
- Add the lime zest and lime juice to the cooked rice. The zest provides a burst of flavor, while the lime juice adds brightness.

Mix in Cilantro:
- Gently fold in the finely chopped cilantro, ensuring it is evenly distributed throughout the rice.

Adjust Seasoning:
- Taste the Cilantro Lime Rice and adjust the seasoning, adding more salt or lime juice if needed.

Serve:
- Serve the Cilantro Lime Rice as a side dish to complement various main courses.

Enjoy:

- Enjoy this flavorful and aromatic Cilantro Lime Rice as a versatile accompaniment to your favorite Mexican, Asian, or other dishes.

This Cilantro Lime Rice recipe is a simple and tasty way to elevate plain rice. The combination of cilantro and lime adds a fresh and vibrant flavor, making it a perfect side dish for a variety of meals. Adjust the lime and cilantro quantities based on your taste preferences.

Lime Infused Quinoa

Ingredients:

- 1 cup quinoa, rinsed and drained
- 2 cups water or vegetable broth
- Zest and juice of 2 limes
- 1 tablespoon olive oil
- 1/2 teaspoon salt
- Fresh cilantro, chopped (for garnish, optional)

Instructions:

Rinse Quinoa:
- Rinse the quinoa under cold water in a fine-mesh sieve until the water runs clear. This helps remove the natural bitterness from the quinoa.

Toast Quinoa (Optional):
- In a dry saucepan over medium heat, toast the rinsed quinoa for 2-3 minutes until it starts to smell nutty. This step is optional but can enhance the nutty flavor of the quinoa.

Cook Quinoa:
- Add the water or vegetable broth, olive oil, lime zest, and salt to the saucepan with the quinoa. Bring to a boil.

Simmer:
- Reduce the heat to low, cover the saucepan, and simmer for 15-20 minutes or until the liquid is absorbed and the quinoa is tender.

Fluff Quinoa:
- Remove the saucepan from heat and let it sit, covered, for 5 minutes. Fluff the quinoa with a fork to separate the grains.

Add Lime Juice:
- Squeeze the juice of the limes over the cooked quinoa. The lime juice adds a bright and citrusy flavor.

Garnish (Optional):
- Garnish the Lime-Infused Quinoa with chopped fresh cilantro for added freshness and color.

Serve:
- Serve the quinoa as a side dish or as a base for salads, bowls, or other main courses.

Enjoy:

- Enjoy this Lime-Infused Quinoa for a flavorful and nutritious addition to your meals.

This Lime-Infused Quinoa recipe is a simple and refreshing way to prepare quinoa with a burst of citrusy flavor. It's a versatile side dish that pairs well with various cuisines and can be used in a variety of recipes. Adjust the lime quantity based on your taste preferences.

Lime and Coconut Sweet Potato Mash

Ingredients:

- 2 large sweet potatoes, peeled and diced
- 1/4 cup coconut milk
- Zest and juice of 1 lime
- 2 tablespoons unsweetened shredded coconut
- 2 tablespoons unsalted butter or coconut oil
- Salt and black pepper, to taste
- Chopped fresh cilantro (for garnish, optional)

Instructions:

Boil Sweet Potatoes:
- Place the diced sweet potatoes in a pot of boiling water. Cook for 15-20 minutes or until the sweet potatoes are fork-tender.

Drain and Mash:
- Drain the cooked sweet potatoes and transfer them to a large bowl. Mash them with a potato masher or fork until smooth.

Add Coconut Milk and Lime:
- Pour in the coconut milk, lime zest, and lime juice. Mix well to combine.

Incorporate Coconut and Butter:
- Add the shredded coconut and unsalted butter or coconut oil to the sweet potatoes. Continue mashing and stirring until the ingredients are well incorporated.

Season:
- Season the Lime and Coconut Sweet Potato Mash with salt and black pepper to taste. Adjust the seasoning according to your preference.

Garnish (Optional):
- If desired, garnish the sweet potato mash with chopped fresh cilantro for added freshness and color.

Serve:
- Serve the Lime and Coconut Sweet Potato Mash as a delightful side dish for your meals.

Enjoy:
- Enjoy this unique and flavorful sweet potato mash with the tropical combination of lime and coconut.

This Lime and Coconut Sweet Potato Mash offers a delicious twist to the classic side dish. The addition of coconut milk, lime zest, and shredded coconut creates a tropical and refreshing flavor profile that pairs well with the natural sweetness of sweet potatoes. Adjust the coconut and lime quantities based on your taste preferences.

Soups:

Lime Chicken Tortilla Soup

Ingredients:

For the Soup:

- 1 pound boneless, skinless chicken breasts or thighs, cooked and shredded
- 1 tablespoon olive oil
- 1 onion, diced
- 3 cloves garlic, minced
- 1 jalapeño, seeds removed and diced
- 1 teaspoon ground cumin
- 1 teaspoon chili powder
- 1/2 teaspoon paprika
- 1 can (14 oz) diced tomatoes
- 4 cups chicken broth
- 1 cup corn kernels (fresh, frozen, or canned)
- 1 cup black beans, drained and rinsed
- Salt and black pepper, to taste

For Serving:

- Lime wedges
- Avocado slices
- Fresh cilantro, chopped
- Tortilla strips or chips
- Shredded cheese
- Sour cream (optional)

Instructions:

Cook and Shred Chicken:
- Cook the chicken breasts or thighs until fully cooked. Shred the chicken and set aside.

Sauté Aromatics:

- In a large pot, heat olive oil over medium heat. Add diced onion, minced garlic, and diced jalapeño. Sauté until the vegetables are softened.

Add Spices:
- Stir in ground cumin, chili powder, and paprika. Cook for an additional 1-2 minutes to toast the spices.

Combine Tomatoes and Broth:
- Add diced tomatoes (with their juice) and chicken broth to the pot. Bring the mixture to a simmer.

Add Corn and Black Beans:
- Add corn kernels and drained black beans to the pot. Stir well.

Simmer:
- Allow the soup to simmer for about 15-20 minutes, allowing the flavors to meld.

Add Shredded Chicken:
- Add the shredded chicken to the soup. Season with salt and black pepper to taste.

Adjust Consistency:
- If the soup is too thick, you can add more chicken broth to reach your desired consistency.

Serve:
- Ladle the Lime Chicken Tortilla Soup into bowls.

Garnish:
- Garnish the soup with lime wedges, avocado slices, chopped fresh cilantro, tortilla strips or chips, and shredded cheese. Add a dollop of sour cream if desired.

Enjoy:
- Serve the Lime Chicken Tortilla Soup hot and enjoy the vibrant flavors.

This Lime Chicken Tortilla Soup is a hearty and flavorful dish with a zesty twist. The lime adds a bright and citrusy flavor that complements the rich broth and tender shredded chicken. Customize your toppings based on your preferences, and don't forget to squeeze fresh lime juice over the soup before enjoying.

Spicy Lime and Black Bean Soup

Ingredients:

- 2 cans (15 oz each) black beans, drained and rinsed
- 1 tablespoon olive oil
- 1 onion, finely chopped
- 3 cloves garlic, minced
- 1 jalapeño, seeds removed and diced
- 1 teaspoon ground cumin
- 1 teaspoon chili powder
- 1/2 teaspoon cayenne pepper (adjust to taste)
- 1 can (14 oz) diced tomatoes
- 4 cups vegetable broth
- Zest and juice of 2 limes
- Salt and black pepper, to taste
- Fresh cilantro, chopped (for garnish)
- Avocado slices (for garnish)
- Sour cream or Greek yogurt (optional, for serving)

Instructions:

Sauté Aromatics:
- In a large pot, heat olive oil over medium heat. Add chopped onion, minced garlic, and diced jalapeño. Sauté until the vegetables are softened.

Add Spices:
- Stir in ground cumin, chili powder, and cayenne pepper. Cook for an additional 1-2 minutes to toast the spices.

Combine Black Beans and Tomatoes:
- Add drained and rinsed black beans, diced tomatoes (with their juice), and vegetable broth to the pot. Stir well.

Simmer:
- Allow the soup to come to a simmer. Let it simmer for about 15-20 minutes to allow the flavors to meld.

Blend Soup (Optional):
- For a smoother consistency, you can use an immersion blender to partially blend the soup. Alternatively, transfer a portion of the soup to a blender, blend until smooth, and return it to the pot.

Add Lime Zest and Juice:
- Stir in the lime zest and lime juice. Season with salt and black pepper to taste.

Adjust Spiciness:
- Taste the soup and adjust the spiciness by adding more cayenne pepper if desired.

Serve:
- Ladle the Spicy Lime and Black Bean Soup into bowls.

Garnish:
- Garnish the soup with chopped fresh cilantro and avocado slices. Add a dollop of sour cream or Greek yogurt if desired.

Enjoy:
- Serve the Spicy Lime and Black Bean Soup hot, and enjoy the bold and zesty flavors.

This Spicy Lime and Black Bean Soup is a satisfying and flavorful dish with a kick of spice and a burst of citrusy lime. It's perfect for warming up on chilly days. Customize the level of spiciness to suit your taste preferences and top it with your favorite garnishes for added texture and freshness.

Thai Coconut Lime Soup

Ingredients:

- 1 pound boneless, skinless chicken thighs, thinly sliced
- 4 cups chicken broth
- 1 can (14 oz) coconut milk
- 1 stalk lemongrass, bruised and chopped into 2-inch pieces
- 3-4 kaffir lime leaves, torn
- 1 inch galangal or ginger, sliced
- 3 tablespoons fish sauce
- 1 tablespoon soy sauce
- 1 tablespoon coconut sugar or brown sugar
- 1 cup button mushrooms, sliced
- 1 medium-sized tomato, cut into wedges
- 1 small onion, thinly sliced
- 2-3 Thai bird chilies, sliced (adjust to spice preference)
- Zest and juice of 2 limes
- Fresh cilantro, chopped (for garnish)
- Thai basil leaves (for garnish)
- Cooked jasmine rice (optional, for serving)

Instructions:

Prepare Ingredients:
- Slice chicken thighs thinly. Bruise the lemongrass by lightly pounding it with the back of a knife. Tear the kaffir lime leaves. Slice galangal or ginger.

Simmer Broth:
- In a large pot, bring chicken broth to a simmer over medium heat.

Add Aromatics:
- Add lemongrass, kaffir lime leaves, and galangal or ginger to the simmering broth. Let it infuse for 5-7 minutes.

Add Chicken:
- Add sliced chicken thighs to the pot and cook until they are no longer pink.

Pour Coconut Milk:
- Pour in the coconut milk, stirring to combine with the broth.

Season the Soup:

- Add fish sauce, soy sauce, and coconut sugar or brown sugar to the pot. Stir well to blend the flavors.

Add Vegetables:
- Add sliced mushrooms, tomato wedges, and thinly sliced onion to the soup. Simmer until the vegetables are tender.

Spice it Up:
- Add sliced Thai bird chilies for spiciness. Adjust the amount based on your spice preference.

Zest and Lime Juice:
- Stir in the lime zest and lime juice for a burst of citrusy flavor.

Taste and Adjust:
- Taste the soup and adjust the seasoning, adding more fish sauce, lime juice, or sugar if needed.

Serve:
- Ladle the Thai Coconut Lime Soup into bowls. Optionally, serve over cooked jasmine rice.

Garnish:
- Garnish with chopped fresh cilantro and Thai basil leaves.

Enjoy:
- Enjoy this authentic and flavorful Thai Coconut Lime Soup (Tom Kha Gai) as a comforting and aromatic meal.

This Thai Coconut Lime Soup is a classic Thai dish known for its rich and aromatic flavors. The combination of lemongrass, kaffir lime, coconut milk, and Thai spices creates a harmonious and comforting soup. Serve it as a standalone soup or over jasmine rice for a complete meal. Adjust the level of spice and sweetness according to your taste preferences.

Avocado Lime Gazpacho

Ingredients:

- 3 ripe avocados, peeled and pitted
- 4 large tomatoes, diced
- 1 cucumber, peeled and diced
- 1 bell pepper (red or yellow), diced
- 1 small red onion, diced
- 2 cloves garlic, minced
- 4 cups vegetable broth
- 1/4 cup fresh cilantro, chopped
- 1/4 cup fresh parsley, chopped
- Zest and juice of 2 limes
- 2 tablespoons red wine vinegar
- 1/4 cup extra-virgin olive oil
- Salt and black pepper, to taste
- Optional toppings: diced avocado, croutons, chopped cilantro

Instructions:

Prepare Vegetables:
- Dice the avocados, tomatoes, cucumber, bell pepper, and red onion.

Blend Avocado Mixture:
- In a blender or food processor, combine avocados, tomatoes, cucumber, bell pepper, red onion, and minced garlic. Blend until smooth.

Add Broth and Herbs:
- Pour in the vegetable broth and blend again until well combined. Add chopped cilantro and parsley to the mixture.

Season:
- Add lime zest, lime juice, red wine vinegar, and extra-virgin olive oil to the blended mixture. Season with salt and black pepper to taste.

Chill:
- Transfer the gazpacho to a large bowl and refrigerate for at least 2 hours to allow the flavors to meld.

Adjust Consistency:
- If the gazpacho is too thick, you can add more vegetable broth to achieve your desired consistency.

Serve:
- Ladle the chilled Avocado Lime Gazpacho into bowls.

Garnish:
- Garnish with additional diced avocado, croutons, and chopped cilantro if desired.

Enjoy:
- Serve this refreshing and creamy Avocado Lime Gazpacho as a cool and vibrant appetizer or light meal.

This Avocado Lime Gazpacho is a delicious twist on the classic cold soup, bringing together the creaminess of avocados with the freshness of lime and a medley of vegetables. It's a perfect dish for hot summer days, providing a burst of flavors and nutrients. Customize the toppings and adjust the seasonings to suit your taste preferences.

Beverages:

Classic Lime Margarita

Ingredients:

- 2 oz silver tequila
- 1 oz triple sec or orange liqueur
- 3/4 oz fresh lime juice
- 1/2 oz simple syrup (adjust to taste)
- Ice
- Salt (for rimming the glass, optional)
- Lime wheel or wedge (for garnish)

Instructions:

Prepare Glass:
- If desired, rim the glass with salt. To do this, moisten the rim of the glass with a lime wedge and dip it into salt.

Fill Glass with Ice:
- Fill the glass with ice cubes to chill it.

Combine Ingredients:
- In a shaker, combine tequila, triple sec, fresh lime juice, and simple syrup.

Shake:
- Shake the mixture well for about 10-15 seconds to chill the ingredients.

Strain into Glass:
- Strain the margarita mixture into the prepared glass over the ice.

Garnish:
- Garnish the drink with a lime wheel or wedge on the rim of the glass.

Enjoy:
- Sip and enjoy the refreshing and classic flavor of the Lime Margarita!

Note:

- Tequila Choice: Use a good quality silver or blanco tequila for a classic margarita.
- Triple Sec: You can also use Cointreau or another orange liqueur.

- Simple Syrup: Adjust the amount of simple syrup based on your sweetness preference.
- Fresh Lime Juice: Always use fresh lime juice for the best flavor.

This Classic Lime Margarita recipe provides a simple and delicious way to enjoy this iconic cocktail. The balance of tequila, triple sec, and fresh lime juice creates a refreshing and tangy drink. Adjust the sweetness and strength according to your taste preferences. Cheers!

Sparkling Cucumber Limeade

Ingredients:

- 1 cucumber, thinly sliced
- 1 cup fresh lime juice (about 6-8 limes)
- 1/2 cup simple syrup (adjust to taste)
- 4 cups sparkling water or club soda
- Ice cubes
- Fresh mint leaves (for garnish)
- Lime slices (for garnish)

Simple Syrup:

- 1/2 cup water
- 1/2 cup granulated sugar

Instructions:

Make Simple Syrup:
- In a small saucepan, combine water and sugar. Heat over medium heat, stirring occasionally, until the sugar dissolves. Remove from heat and let it cool. This is your simple syrup.

Prepare Cucumber and Lime Juice:
- Thinly slice the cucumber. Squeeze the limes to extract fresh lime juice.

Combine Ingredients:
- In a large pitcher, combine cucumber slices, fresh lime juice, and simple syrup.

Muddle (Optional):
- If you prefer a more pronounced cucumber flavor, you can muddle the cucumber slices in the pitcher to release their juices.

Add Sparkling Water:
- Pour the sparkling water or club soda into the pitcher and stir gently to combine.

Taste and Adjust:
- Taste the Sparkling Cucumber Limeade and adjust the sweetness by adding more simple syrup if needed.

Chill:

- Place the pitcher in the refrigerator to chill for at least 1-2 hours.

Serve:
- Fill glasses with ice cubes and pour the chilled Sparkling Cucumber Limeade.

Garnish:
- Garnish each glass with fresh mint leaves and lime slices.

Enjoy:
- Refresh yourself with this Sparkling Cucumber Limeade, a delightful and hydrating beverage.

Note:

- Customization: Feel free to customize the sweetness and adjust the ratio of lime juice and cucumber to suit your taste.
- Variations: You can add a splash of elderflower liqueur or mint syrup for added complexity.

This Sparkling Cucumber Limeade is a light and effervescent drink perfect for warm days. The combination of cucumber, lime, and sparkling water creates a refreshing and hydrating beverage. Adjust the sweetness to your liking and enjoy this delightful and stylish drink.

Minty Lime Mojito

Ingredients:

- 2 oz white rum
- 1 oz fresh lime juice (about 1-2 limes)
- 2 teaspoons sugar (adjust to taste)
- 8-10 fresh mint leaves, plus extra for garnish
- Soda water or club soda
- Ice cubes
- Lime slices (for garnish)

Instructions:

Muddle Mint and Sugar:
- In a glass, muddle the fresh mint leaves and sugar together. Muddle gently to release the mint's flavor without tearing the leaves.

Add Lime Juice:
- Squeeze fresh lime juice into the glass over the muddled mint and sugar.

Add Rum:
- Pour the white rum into the glass.

Fill with Ice:
- Fill the glass with ice cubes.

Stir:
- Stir the ingredients well to mix the mint, sugar, lime juice, and rum.

Top with Soda Water:
- Top up the glass with soda water or club soda. Leave some space at the top for stirring.

Stir Again:
- Gently stir the Mojito to combine all the ingredients.

Garnish:
- Garnish the drink with fresh mint leaves and lime slices.

Enjoy:
- Sip and enjoy the Minty Lime Mojito, a classic and refreshing cocktail.

Note:

- Adjust Sweetness: Taste the Mojito and adjust the sweetness by adding more sugar if needed.

- Mint Flavor: If you prefer a stronger mint flavor, you can muddle more mint leaves or slap them between your hands before adding to release their aroma.

This Minty Lime Mojito is a classic cocktail that combines the zesty freshness of lime with the coolness of mint and the kick of white rum. It's a perfect drink to enjoy on a warm day or to cool off after a long week. Adjust the ingredients to suit your taste preferences and elevate your cocktail experience. Cheers!

Ginger Lime Iced Tea

Ingredients:

- 4 cups water
- 4 black tea bags (or your favorite tea)
- 1-2 inches fresh ginger, peeled and sliced
- 1/4 cup honey or sweetener of choice (adjust to taste)
- 1/2 cup fresh lime juice (about 4-6 limes)
- Ice cubes
- Lime slices and fresh mint leaves (for garnish, optional)

Instructions:

Boil Water:
- Bring 4 cups of water to a boil in a saucepan.

Steep Tea:
- Remove the saucepan from heat and add the tea bags and sliced ginger. Let it steep for 5-7 minutes, or according to the tea package instructions.

Sweeten:
- While the tea is still warm, stir in honey or your sweetener of choice. Adjust the sweetness to your liking.

Cool:
- Allow the tea to cool to room temperature. You can speed up the process by placing it in the refrigerator.

Add Lime Juice:
- Once the tea is cool, add fresh lime juice and stir well.

Strain (Optional):
- If you prefer a smoother texture, you can strain the tea to remove the tea bags and ginger slices.

Chill:
- Refrigerate the ginger lime tea for at least 1-2 hours to ensure it is thoroughly chilled.

Serve Over Ice:
- Fill glasses with ice cubes and pour the chilled ginger lime tea over the ice.

Garnish (Optional):
- Garnish with lime slices and fresh mint leaves for a refreshing touch.

Enjoy:

- Sip and enjoy the invigorating flavor of Ginger Lime Iced Tea on a hot day.

Note:

- Variations: Experiment with different tea varieties such as green tea or herbal tea for unique flavors.
- Adjust Ingredients: Feel free to adjust the ginger, lime, and sweetness levels based on your preferences.

This Ginger Lime Iced Tea is a delightful and refreshing beverage with a perfect balance of ginger's warmth and lime's zesty brightness. It's a great way to cool down and enjoy a flavorful iced tea. Customize the sweetness and garnishes to suit your taste.

Watermelon Lime Slush

Ingredients:

- 4 cups seedless watermelon, cubed
- 1/4 cup fresh lime juice (about 2-3 limes)
- 2 tablespoons honey or agave syrup (adjust to taste)
- 2 cups ice cubes
- Mint leaves for garnish (optional)
- Lime slices for garnish (optional)

Instructions:

Prepare Watermelon:
- Cut the seedless watermelon into small cubes, removing any seeds.

Freeze Watermelon:
- Place the watermelon cubes in a single layer on a tray or plate. Freeze for at least 2 hours or until solid.

Blend Ingredients:
- In a blender, combine the frozen watermelon cubes, fresh lime juice, and honey or agave syrup.

Blend Until Smooth:
- Blend the ingredients until you achieve a smooth and slushy consistency.

Adjust Sweetness:
- Taste the slush and adjust the sweetness by adding more honey or agave syrup if needed.

Serve:
- Pour the Watermelon Lime Slush into glasses.

Garnish (Optional):
- Garnish with mint leaves and lime slices for a fresh and vibrant presentation.

Enjoy:
- Sip and enjoy the cool and refreshing Watermelon Lime Slush on a hot day!

Note:

- Variations: Add a splash of sparkling water for a fizzy twist or a hint of ginger for extra flavor.
- Minty Twist: Blend fresh mint leaves with the slush for a mint-infused version.

This Watermelon Lime Slush is a delicious and hydrating treat that's perfect for staying cool in warm weather. The natural sweetness of watermelon combined with the citrusy zing of lime creates a refreshing beverage. Customize the sweetness and add your favorite garnishes for an extra touch of flavor.

Desserts:

Key Lime Pie

Ingredients:

For the Graham Cracker Crust:

- 1 1/2 cups graham cracker crumbs
- 1/3 cup sugar
- 1/2 cup unsalted butter, melted

For the Key Lime Filling:

- 3/4 cup key lime juice (about 15-20 key limes)
- 2 teaspoons key lime zest
- 3 large egg yolks
- 1 can (14 ounces) sweetened condensed milk

For the Whipped Cream Topping:

- 1 cup heavy cream
- 2 tablespoons sugar
- 1 teaspoon vanilla extract

Instructions:

Preheat Oven:
- Preheat your oven to 350°F (175°C).

Make Graham Cracker Crust:
- In a bowl, combine graham cracker crumbs, sugar, and melted butter. Press the mixture into the bottom and up the sides of a 9-inch pie dish.

Bake Crust:
- Bake the crust in the preheated oven for 8-10 minutes or until lightly golden. Allow it to cool while preparing the filling.

Prepare Key Lime Filling:
- In a mixing bowl, whisk together key lime juice, key lime zest, egg yolks, and sweetened condensed milk until well combined.

Pour Filling into Crust:

- Pour the key lime filling into the cooled graham cracker crust.

Bake Pie:
- Bake the pie in the preheated oven for 15-20 minutes or until the filling is set. It should still have a slight jiggle in the center.

Chill:
- Allow the pie to cool to room temperature, then refrigerate for at least 4 hours or preferably overnight.

Make Whipped Cream Topping:
- In a separate bowl, whip the heavy cream, sugar, and vanilla extract until stiff peaks form.

Serve:
- Spread the whipped cream over the chilled key lime pie.

Garnish (Optional):
- Garnish with additional key lime zest or slices.

Slice and Enjoy:
- Slice the Key Lime Pie and enjoy the tangy and sweet flavors!

Note:

- Key Lime Substitution: If key limes are not available, you can use regular limes for the juice and zest.
- Store: Keep the Key Lime Pie refrigerated. It can be stored for several days.

This Key Lime Pie recipe delivers a perfect balance of tartness and sweetness, with a smooth and creamy texture. The graham cracker crust adds a delightful crunch, and the whipped cream topping provides a light and airy finish. It's a classic dessert that captures the essence of key lime flavor.

Coconut Lime Bars

Ingredients:

For the Crust:

- 1 cup all-purpose flour
- 1/2 cup powdered sugar
- 1/2 cup unsalted butter, softened

For the Coconut Lime Filling:

- 1 cup shredded coconut (sweetened or unsweetened)
- 3 large eggs
- 1 1/2 cups granulated sugar
- 1/2 cup all-purpose flour
- 1/2 teaspoon baking powder
- 1/4 teaspoon salt
- Zest of 2 limes
- 1/2 cup fresh lime juice (about 4-6 limes)

For the Topping:

- Powdered sugar for dusting (optional)
- Lime slices or zest for garnish (optional)

Instructions:

Preheat Oven:
- Preheat your oven to 350°F (175°C). Grease and line a 9x9-inch square baking pan with parchment paper, leaving an overhang for easy removal.

Make the Crust:
- In a bowl, combine the flour, powdered sugar, and softened butter. Mix until crumbly. Press the mixture into the bottom of the prepared baking pan.

Bake the Crust:

- Bake the crust in the preheated oven for 15-18 minutes or until lightly golden. Remove from the oven and let it cool slightly.

Prepare Coconut Lime Filling:
- In a separate bowl, whisk together shredded coconut, eggs, granulated sugar, flour, baking powder, salt, lime zest, and lime juice until well combined.

Pour Filling Over Crust:
- Pour the coconut lime filling over the partially baked crust.

Bake Bars:
- Return the pan to the oven and bake for an additional 20-25 minutes or until the edges are golden and the center is set.

Cool Completely:
- Allow the bars to cool completely in the pan on a wire rack.

Chill (Optional):
- For easier slicing, you can chill the bars in the refrigerator for a couple of hours.

Slice:
- Once cooled, use the parchment paper overhang to lift the bars from the pan. Place on a cutting board and slice into squares or bars.

Dust with Powdered Sugar (Optional):
- Dust the tops of the bars with powdered sugar if desired.

Garnish (Optional):
- Garnish with lime slices or zest for a decorative touch.

Serve and Enjoy:
- Serve these Coconut Lime Bars and enjoy the delightful combination of coconut and lime flavors!

Note:

- Storage: Store the bars in an airtight container in the refrigerator for freshness.
- Variation: If you prefer a toasted coconut flavor, you can toast the shredded coconut before adding it to the filling mixture.

Lime Sorbet

Ingredients:

- 1 cup fresh lime juice (about 8-10 limes)
- Zest of 2 limes
- 1 cup granulated sugar
- 2 cups water

Instructions:

Prepare Lime Juice:
- Squeeze enough limes to yield 1 cup of fresh lime juice. Zest two of the limes for additional flavor.

Make Simple Syrup:
- In a saucepan, combine 1 cup of water and 1 cup of granulated sugar. Heat over medium heat, stirring until the sugar is completely dissolved. Remove from heat and let the simple syrup cool.

Combine Lime Juice and Zest:
- In a mixing bowl, combine the fresh lime juice and lime zest.

Mix Simple Syrup:
- Once the simple syrup has cooled, add it to the lime juice and zest mixture. Stir well to combine.

Chill Mixture:
- Place the lime mixture in the refrigerator and let it chill for at least 2 hours or until it's thoroughly cold.

Freeze in Ice Cream Maker:
- Transfer the chilled lime mixture to an ice cream maker and churn according to the manufacturer's instructions.

Alternative Freezing Method:
- If you don't have an ice cream maker, pour the mixture into a shallow, freezer-safe dish. Place it in the freezer. Every 30 minutes, stir the mixture with a fork to break up any ice crystals. Repeat until the sorbet reaches your desired consistency.

Final Freeze:
- Once the sorbet has reached a slushy texture in the ice cream maker or the desired consistency through manual freezing, transfer it to a lidded container and freeze for an additional 2-4 hours to firm up.

Serve:
- Scoop the Lime Sorbet into bowls or cones and serve immediately.

Garnish (Optional):
- Garnish with additional lime zest or a slice of lime for a decorative touch.

Enjoy:
- Enjoy the refreshing and tangy taste of homemade Lime Sorbet!

Note:

- Storage: Store any leftover sorbet in an airtight container in the freezer. Let it soften for a few minutes before scooping if it becomes too hard.

This Homemade Lime Sorbet is a simple and refreshing treat with a burst of citrus flavor. It's perfect for cooling down on a hot day or as a palate cleanser between courses. Customize the sweetness to your liking and enjoy this delightful, homemade frozen dessert.

Lime Cheesecake

Ingredients:

For the Crust:

- 1 1/2 cups graham cracker crumbs
- 1/4 cup granulated sugar
- 1/2 cup unsalted butter, melted

For the Lime Cheesecake Filling:

- 4 packages (8 oz each) cream cheese, softened
- 1 1/4 cups granulated sugar
- 4 large eggs
- 1 cup sour cream
- 1/4 cup all-purpose flour
- Zest of 3 limes
- 1/2 cup fresh lime juice (about 4-6 limes)

For the Lime Glaze (Optional):

- 1/2 cup powdered sugar
- 2 tablespoons fresh lime juice
- Lime zest for garnish

Instructions:

Preheat Oven:
- Preheat your oven to 325°F (163°C). Grease a 9-inch springform pan.

Make the Crust:
- In a bowl, combine graham cracker crumbs, sugar, and melted butter. Press the mixture into the bottom of the prepared springform pan to create the crust.

Bake the Crust:
- Bake the crust in the preheated oven for 10 minutes. Remove from the oven and allow it to cool while preparing the filling.

Prepare Lime Cheesecake Filling:

- In a large mixing bowl, beat the softened cream cheese and sugar together until smooth. Add the eggs one at a time, beating well after each addition.

Add Sour Cream and Flour:
- Mix in the sour cream and flour until well combined.

Add Lime Zest and Juice:
- Add the lime zest and fresh lime juice to the cream cheese mixture. Mix until the filling is smooth and well incorporated.

Pour Filling Over Crust:
- Pour the lime cheesecake filling over the prepared crust in the springform pan.

Bake Cheesecake:
- Bake the cheesecake in the preheated oven for about 55-60 minutes or until the center is set and the edges are lightly browned.

Cool and Chill:
- Allow the cheesecake to cool in the oven with the door ajar for about an hour. Then, refrigerate for at least 4 hours or overnight to allow it to set completely.

Make Lime Glaze (Optional):
- In a small bowl, whisk together powdered sugar and lime juice to create a glaze.

Glaze Cheesecake (Optional):
- Drizzle the lime glaze over the chilled cheesecake. Garnish with additional lime zest if desired.

Slice and Serve:
- Release the sides of the springform pan and slice the Lime Cheesecake into servings.

Enjoy:
- Enjoy the tangy and creamy goodness of this delightful Lime Cheesecake!

Note:

- Lime Zest Tip: For the best flavor, make sure to zest the limes before juicing.
- Chilling Time: Allowing the cheesecake to chill thoroughly ensures a firm and creamy texture.

This Lime Cheesecake is a luscious and zesty dessert that combines the rich creaminess of classic cheesecake with the vibrant flavors of fresh lime. Whether enjoyed plain or with a lime glaze, it's a perfect treat for lime lovers and a refreshing choice for any occasion.

Margarita Cupcakes

Ingredients:

For the Cupcakes:

- 1 1/2 cups all-purpose flour
- 1 1/2 teaspoons baking powder
- 1/4 teaspoon salt
- 1/2 cup unsalted butter, softened
- 1 cup granulated sugar
- 2 large eggs
- 1 teaspoon vanilla extract
- 1/2 cup whole milk
- 1/4 cup tequila
- 2 tablespoons lime juice
- Zest of 2 limes

For the Tequila-Lime Frosting:

- 1 cup unsalted butter, softened
- 4 cups powdered sugar
- 2 tablespoons tequila
- 1 tablespoon lime juice
- Zest of 1 lime
- Pinch of salt (optional)

For Garnish (Optional):

- Coarse salt for rimming
- Lime slices or wedges

Instructions:

Preheat Oven:
- Preheat your oven to 350°F (175°C). Line a cupcake tin with paper liners.

Make Cupcake Batter:
- In a bowl, whisk together flour, baking powder, and salt. In another bowl, cream together softened butter and granulated sugar until light and fluffy.

- Add eggs one at a time, beating well after each addition. Stir in vanilla extract.

Add Dry Ingredients:
- Gradually add the dry ingredients to the wet ingredients, alternating with the milk. Begin and end with the dry ingredients. Mix until just combined.

Incorporate Tequila and Lime:
- Stir in tequila, lime juice, and lime zest until evenly distributed in the batter.

Fill Cupcake Liners:
- Spoon the batter into the cupcake liners, filling each about 2/3 full.

Bake Cupcakes:
- Bake in the preheated oven for 18-20 minutes or until a toothpick inserted into the center comes out clean. Allow the cupcakes to cool completely.

Make Tequila-Lime Frosting:
- In a mixing bowl, beat softened butter until creamy. Gradually add powdered sugar and continue to beat until smooth. Mix in tequila, lime juice, lime zest, and a pinch of salt if desired. Beat until the frosting is light and fluffy.

Frost Cupcakes:
- Once the cupcakes are completely cooled, frost them with the Tequila-Lime Frosting.

Optional Garnish:
- Optionally, rim the edges of the cupcakes with coarse salt. Garnish with lime slices or wedges.

Serve and Enjoy:
- Serve these Margarita Cupcakes and enjoy the festive and citrusy flavors!

Note:

- Adjust Tequila: If you want a more pronounced tequila flavor, you can add an extra tablespoon to the frosting.
- Rimming the Edges: If rimming the edges with salt, moisten the edges of the cupcakes with a little lime juice before dipping them into the salt.

These Margarita Cupcakes capture the essence of a classic margarita in a delightful dessert form. The combination of tequila and lime creates a zesty and refreshing flavor, making them a perfect treat for celebrations or any day you want to add a touch of fun to your dessert. Cheers!

Lime and Coconut Panna Cotta

Ingredients:

For the Panna Cotta:

- 2 cups coconut milk
- 1 cup heavy cream
- 1/2 cup granulated sugar
- Zest of 2 limes
- 1 teaspoon vanilla extract
- 2 tablespoons cold water
- 2 teaspoons unflavored gelatin

For the Lime Jelly:

- 1/2 cup fresh lime juice (about 4-6 limes)
- 1/4 cup granulated sugar
- 1 teaspoon unflavored gelatin
- 2 tablespoons cold water

For Garnish (Optional):

- Shredded coconut
- Lime zest
- Fresh mint leaves

Instructions:

Prepare Panna Cotta Base:
- In a saucepan, combine coconut milk, heavy cream, granulated sugar, lime zest, and vanilla extract. Heat over medium heat, stirring occasionally until the sugar is dissolved. Remove from heat.

Bloom Gelatin:
- In a small bowl, sprinkle the unflavored gelatin over 2 tablespoons of cold water. Let it sit for a few minutes to bloom.

Add Gelatin to Panna Cotta Mixture:

- Add the bloomed gelatin to the warm coconut milk mixture. Stir until the gelatin is completely dissolved.

Strain Mixture:
- Strain the panna cotta mixture through a fine-mesh sieve into a bowl to remove the lime zest. This ensures a smooth texture.

Pour into Molds:
- Pour the panna cotta mixture into individual molds or glasses, filling them about 2/3 of the way. Refrigerate for at least 4 hours or until set.

Prepare Lime Jelly:
- In a small saucepan, combine fresh lime juice and granulated sugar. Heat over medium heat until the sugar is dissolved. Remove from heat.

Bloom Gelatin for Lime Jelly:
- In a small bowl, sprinkle the unflavored gelatin over 2 tablespoons of cold water. Let it sit for a few minutes to bloom.

Add Gelatin to Lime Juice Mixture:
- Add the bloomed gelatin to the warm lime juice mixture. Stir until the gelatin is completely dissolved.

Cool Lime Jelly:
- Allow the lime jelly mixture to cool to room temperature.

Pour Lime Jelly Over Set Panna Cotta:
- Once the panna cotta is set, pour the cooled lime jelly over the top of each mold or glass.

Chill:
- Return the molds or glasses to the refrigerator and chill for an additional 2-4 hours or until the lime jelly is set.

Garnish and Serve:
- Garnish with shredded coconut, lime zest, and fresh mint leaves if desired. Serve and enjoy the delightful Lime and Coconut Panna Cotta!

Note:

- Mold Options: You can use ramekins, glasses, or silicone molds for shaping the panna cotta.
- Adjust Sweetness: Adjust the amount of sugar in the lime jelly according to your sweetness preference.

This Lime and Coconut Panna Cotta combines the tropical flavors of coconut and the zesty brightness of lime in a smooth and creamy dessert. The addition of a lime jelly layer adds an extra burst of citrus flavor. It's an elegant and refreshing treat that's perfect for special occasions or as a delightful ending to a meal.

Lime Posset

Ingredients:

- 2 cups heavy cream
- 3/4 cup granulated sugar
- Zest of 2 limes
- 1/2 cup fresh lime juice (about 4-6 limes)
- Fresh berries or mint leaves for garnish (optional)

Instructions:

Prepare Serving Glasses:
- Arrange serving glasses or ramekins on a tray or in the refrigerator.

Zest and Juice Limes:
- Zest the limes to get the lime zest and then squeeze the limes to obtain fresh lime juice.

Make Lime Cream Mixture:
- In a saucepan, combine heavy cream, granulated sugar, and lime zest. Heat over medium heat, stirring continuously, until the sugar is dissolved and the mixture starts to simmer. Do not let it boil.

Simmer and Remove from Heat:
- Allow the cream mixture to simmer gently for about 3-4 minutes, stirring constantly. Remove from heat.

Add Lime Juice:
- Stir in the fresh lime juice. Continue stirring until well combined.

Strain Mixture:
- Strain the lime cream mixture through a fine-mesh sieve into a bowl to remove the lime zest. This ensures a smooth texture.

Divide and Pour:
- Divide the lime posset mixture evenly among the prepared serving glasses or ramekins.

Chill:
- Place the tray or glasses in the refrigerator and let the lime posset set for at least 4 hours or until fully chilled and firm.

Garnish (Optional):
- Before serving, garnish with fresh berries or mint leaves if desired.

Serve and Enjoy:
- Serve the Lime Posset chilled and enjoy the creamy, citrusy goodness!

Note:

- Make Ahead: Lime Posset can be made a day in advance. Keep it covered in the refrigerator until ready to serve.
- Customize Garnish: Feel free to get creative with the garnish, such as adding a dollop of whipped cream or a sprinkle of grated lime zest.

This Lime Posset is a simple and elegant dessert with a silky texture and a burst of lime flavor. It requires minimal ingredients and effort, making it an excellent choice for a refreshing treat, especially during warmer seasons. Enjoy the delightful combination of creaminess and citrus in every spoonful!

Mango Lime Sorbet

Ingredients:

- 3 cups ripe mango, peeled, pitted, and diced
- 1 cup granulated sugar (adjust to taste)
- 1/2 cup water
- 1/4 cup fresh lime juice (about 2-3 limes)
- Zest of 1 lime
- Pinch of salt

Instructions:

Prepare Mango:
- Peel, pit, and dice ripe mango until you have about 3 cups of mango chunks.

Make Simple Syrup:
- In a small saucepan, combine granulated sugar and water. Heat over medium heat, stirring until the sugar is completely dissolved. Remove from heat and let the simple syrup cool.

Blend Mango:
- In a blender or food processor, puree the diced mango until smooth.

Combine Mango Puree and Simple Syrup:
- In a mixing bowl, combine the mango puree with the cooled simple syrup. Mix well.

Add Lime Juice and Zest:
- Add fresh lime juice and lime zest to the mango mixture. Stir until everything is well combined.

Adjust Sweetness:
- Taste the mixture and adjust the sweetness by adding more sugar if needed. Keep in mind that freezing dulls the sweetness, so it's okay if the mixture tastes slightly sweeter than desired.

Chill Mixture:
- Cover the bowl and refrigerate the mango-lime mixture for at least 2 hours or until thoroughly chilled.

Freeze in Ice Cream Maker:
- Transfer the chilled mixture to an ice cream maker and churn according to the manufacturer's instructions until it reaches a sorbet consistency.

Alternative Freezing Method:

- If you don't have an ice cream maker, pour the mixture into a shallow, freezer-safe dish. Place it in the freezer. Every 30 minutes, stir the mixture with a fork to break up any ice crystals. Repeat until the sorbet reaches your desired consistency.

Final Freeze:
- Once the sorbet has reached a slushy texture in the ice cream maker or the desired consistency through manual freezing, transfer it to a lidded container and freeze for an additional 2-4 hours to firm up.

Serve and Enjoy:
- Scoop the Mango Lime Sorbet into bowls or cones and enjoy the tropical and citrusy flavors!

Note:

- Variations: You can add a splash of rum or vodka to the mixture before freezing for a hint of adult flair.
- Garnish: Garnish the sorbet with fresh mint leaves or additional lime zest for a decorative touch.

This Mango Lime Sorbet is a refreshing and tropical treat that captures the sweetness of ripe mangoes and the zingy brightness of fresh lime. It's a delightful dessert to cool down on a hot day or as a palate cleanser between courses. Enjoy the vibrant flavors of this homemade sorbet!

Baked Goods:

Lime Poppy Seed Muffins

Ingredients:

Dry Ingredients:

- 2 cups all-purpose flour
- 3/4 cup granulated sugar
- 2 tablespoons poppy seeds
- 1 tablespoon lime zest
- 1 teaspoon baking powder
- 1/2 teaspoon baking soda
- 1/4 teaspoon salt

Wet Ingredients:

- 1/2 cup unsalted butter, melted and cooled
- 2/3 cup buttermilk
- 1/4 cup fresh lime juice (about 2-3 limes)
- 2 large eggs
- 1 teaspoon vanilla extract

For the Glaze (Optional):

- 1 cup powdered sugar
- 2 tablespoons fresh lime juice
- Additional lime zest for garnish

Instructions:

Preheat Oven:
- Preheat your oven to 375°F (190°C). Line a muffin tin with paper liners.

Prepare Dry Ingredients:
- In a large mixing bowl, whisk together the flour, sugar, poppy seeds, lime zest, baking powder, baking soda, and salt.

Prepare Wet Ingredients:

- In a separate bowl, whisk together the melted butter, buttermilk, lime juice, eggs, and vanilla extract.

Combine Wet and Dry Ingredients:
- Pour the wet ingredients into the bowl with the dry ingredients. Gently fold and mix until just combined. Do not overmix; it's okay if there are a few lumps.

Fill Muffin Cups:
- Spoon the batter into the prepared muffin cups, filling each about two-thirds full.

Bake Muffins:
- Bake in the preheated oven for 18-20 minutes or until a toothpick inserted into the center comes out clean.

Cool Muffins:
- Allow the muffins to cool in the tin for a few minutes, then transfer them to a wire rack to cool completely.

Prepare Glaze (Optional):
- If using the glaze, whisk together powdered sugar and fresh lime juice until smooth.

Glaze Muffins (Optional):
- Once the muffins are completely cooled, drizzle the glaze over the top. Sprinkle additional lime zest on top for garnish.

Serve and Enjoy:
- Serve these Lime Poppy Seed Muffins and enjoy the citrusy and nutty flavors!

Note:

- Make Ahead: These muffins can be made ahead of time and stored in an airtight container. Glaze them before serving for a fresh look.
- Buttermilk Substitute: If you don't have buttermilk, you can make a substitute by adding 1 teaspoon of white vinegar or lemon juice to 2/3 cup of milk. Let it sit for a few minutes before using.

These Lime Poppy Seed Muffins are a delightful combination of citrus and nutty flavors. The addition of lime zest and juice gives them a refreshing twist, making them a perfect choice for breakfast or a light snack. The optional glaze adds a sweet and tangy finish to these moist and flavorful muffins.

Coconut Lime Drizzle Cake

Ingredients:

For the Cake:

- 1 cup unsalted butter, softened
- 1 cup granulated sugar
- 4 large eggs
- 2 cups all-purpose flour
- 2 teaspoons baking powder
- 1/2 teaspoon salt
- 1 cup shredded coconut (sweetened or unsweetened)
- Zest of 2 limes
- 1/4 cup fresh lime juice (about 2 limes)
- 1/2 cup buttermilk

For the Lime Drizzle:

- 1/4 cup fresh lime juice (about 2 limes)
- 1/2 cup powdered sugar

For Garnish (Optional):

- Shredded coconut
- Lime zest

Instructions:

Preheat Oven:
- Preheat your oven to 350°F (175°C). Grease and line a loaf pan with parchment paper, leaving an overhang for easy removal.

Make the Cake Batter:
- In a large mixing bowl, cream together the softened butter and granulated sugar until light and fluffy. Add the eggs one at a time, beating well after each addition.

Combine Dry Ingredients:

- In a separate bowl, whisk together the flour, baking powder, and salt.

Add Coconut and Lime Zest:
- Add the shredded coconut and lime zest to the dry ingredients. Toss to coat the coconut with flour.

Alternately Add Dry and Wet Ingredients:
- Gradually add the dry ingredients to the creamed butter and sugar, alternating with the buttermilk. Begin and end with the dry ingredients. Mix until just combined.

Add Lime Juice:
- Stir in the fresh lime juice until evenly incorporated into the batter.

Pour Batter into Loaf Pan:
- Pour the batter into the prepared loaf pan, spreading it evenly.

Bake Cake:
- Bake in the preheated oven for 50-60 minutes or until a toothpick inserted into the center comes out clean.

Prepare Lime Drizzle:
- While the cake is baking, prepare the lime drizzle. In a small bowl, whisk together fresh lime juice and powdered sugar until smooth.

Drizzle Cake with Lime Mixture:
- Once the cake is out of the oven and still warm, use a toothpick or skewer to poke holes all over the top. Drizzle the lime mixture over the warm cake, allowing it to soak in.

Cool and Garnish:
- Allow the cake to cool completely in the pan. Once cooled, use the parchment paper overhang to lift the cake from the pan. Garnish with shredded coconut and additional lime zest if desired.

Slice and Serve:
- Slice the Coconut Lime Drizzle Cake and serve. Enjoy the tropical and zesty flavors!

Note:

- Storage: Store any leftovers in an airtight container at room temperature or in the refrigerator, depending on your preference.
- Make Ahead: This cake can be made a day in advance and still maintains its delicious flavor and moisture.

This Coconut Lime Drizzle Cake is a perfect blend of tropical coconut and zesty lime, making it a delightful treat for any occasion. The drizzle adds an extra burst of citrus flavor, and the shredded coconut on top adds a lovely texture. Enjoy a slice with a cup of tea or coffee for a refreshing and flavorful experience.

Lime Zest Shortbread Cookies

Ingredients:

- 1 cup unsalted butter, softened
- 1/2 cup powdered sugar
- 2 cups all-purpose flour
- Zest of 2 limes
- 1/4 teaspoon salt
- Extra powdered sugar for dusting (optional)

Instructions:

Preheat Oven:
- Preheat your oven to 325°F (163°C). Line a baking sheet with parchment paper.

Cream Butter and Sugar:
- In a large bowl, cream together the softened butter and powdered sugar until light and fluffy.

Add Lime Zest:
- Add the lime zest to the butter-sugar mixture. Mix well to incorporate the lime flavor.

Combine Dry Ingredients:
- In a separate bowl, whisk together the all-purpose flour and salt.

Incorporate Dry Ingredients:
- Gradually add the dry ingredients to the butter mixture. Mix until just combined. Be careful not to overmix.

Form Cookie Dough:
- Gather the dough into a ball and flatten it into a disk. Wrap the dough in plastic wrap and chill in the refrigerator for at least 30 minutes.

Roll and Cut Cookies:
- On a floured surface, roll out the chilled dough to a thickness of about 1/4 inch. Use cookie cutters to cut out shapes.

Place on Baking Sheet:
- Place the cut-out cookies on the prepared baking sheet, leaving some space between each cookie.

Chill Again (Optional):

- If time allows, chill the cut-out cookies in the refrigerator for another 15-20 minutes. This helps the cookies maintain their shape during baking.

Bake Cookies:
- Bake in the preheated oven for 12-15 minutes or until the edges are just starting to turn golden.

Cool on Rack:
- Allow the cookies to cool on the baking sheet for a few minutes, then transfer them to a wire rack to cool completely.

Optional Dusting:
- Once cooled, dust the cookies with powdered sugar if desired.

Serve and Enjoy:
- Serve these delightful Lime Zest Shortbread Cookies and enjoy the buttery and citrusy goodness!

Note:

- Storage: Store the cookies in an airtight container at room temperature. They can also be frozen for longer storage.
- Variation: For an extra touch, you can dip the cooled cookies in melted white chocolate and sprinkle with additional lime zest.

These Lime Zest Shortbread Cookies are a melt-in-your-mouth delight with a burst of citrus flavor. The buttery and tender texture combined with the zesty lime make them a perfect treat for any occasion. Enjoy these cookies with a cup of tea or coffee for a delightful snack.

Blueberry Lime Scones

Ingredients:

- 2 cups all-purpose flour
- 1/2 cup granulated sugar
- 1 tablespoon baking powder
- 1/2 teaspoon salt
- 1/2 cup unsalted butter, cold and cut into small cubes
- 1 cup fresh blueberries
- Zest of 2 limes
- 1/2 cup milk (plus extra for brushing)
- 1 large egg
- 1 teaspoon vanilla extract

For the Glaze:

- 1 cup powdered sugar
- 2 tablespoons fresh lime juice
- Zest of 1 lime

Instructions:

Preheat Oven:
- Preheat your oven to 400°F (200°C). Line a baking sheet with parchment paper.

Prepare Dry Ingredients:
- In a large mixing bowl, whisk together the flour, sugar, baking powder, and salt.

Cut in Butter:
- Add the cold, cubed butter to the dry ingredients. Use a pastry cutter or your fingers to cut the butter into the flour mixture until it resembles coarse crumbs.

Add Blueberries and Lime Zest:
- Gently fold in the fresh blueberries and lime zest into the flour-butter mixture.

Combine Wet Ingredients:
- In a separate bowl, whisk together the milk, egg, and vanilla extract.

Form Dough:
- Make a well in the center of the dry ingredients and pour the wet ingredients into it. Mix until just combined. Do not overmix.

Shape and Cut Scones:
- Turn the dough out onto a floured surface and gently knead it a few times. Pat the dough into a circle about 1 inch thick. Use a sharp knife to cut the circle into 8 wedges.

Place on Baking Sheet:
- Transfer the scones to the prepared baking sheet, leaving some space between each wedge.

Brush with Milk:
- Lightly brush the tops of the scones with a little milk.

Bake Scones:
- Bake in the preheated oven for 15-18 minutes or until the scones are golden brown.

Prepare Glaze:
- While the scones are baking, prepare the glaze. Whisk together powdered sugar, fresh lime juice, and lime zest until smooth.

Glaze Scones:
- Once the scones are out of the oven and slightly cooled, drizzle the glaze over the top.

Serve and Enjoy:
- Serve these Blueberry Lime Scones warm or at room temperature. Enjoy the delightful combination of blueberries and lime!

Note:

- Frozen Blueberries: If using frozen blueberries, do not thaw them before adding to the dough. This helps prevent the color from bleeding too much into the scones.
- Storage: Store leftover scones in an airtight container at room temperature for 1-2 days or in the refrigerator for a longer shelf life.

These Blueberry Lime Scones are a perfect blend of sweet blueberries and tangy lime, creating a delicious treat for breakfast or afternoon tea. The tender and flaky texture, along with the citrusy glaze, makes them an irresistible choice. Enjoy these scones with your favorite hot beverage for a delightful snack!

Lime and Pistachio Biscotti

Ingredients:

- 2 cups all-purpose flour
- 1 cup granulated sugar
- 1 teaspoon baking powder
- 1/2 teaspoon salt
- Zest of 2 limes
- 1 cup unsalted pistachios, chopped
- 3 large eggs
- 1 teaspoon vanilla extract
- 2 tablespoons fresh lime juice

For the Glaze:

- 1 cup powdered sugar
- 2 tablespoons fresh lime juice
- Chopped pistachios for garnish (optional)

Instructions:

Preheat Oven:
- Preheat your oven to 350°F (175°C). Line a baking sheet with parchment paper.

Prepare Dry Ingredients:
- In a large mixing bowl, whisk together the flour, sugar, baking powder, and salt.

Add Lime Zest and Pistachios:
- Stir in the lime zest and chopped pistachios into the dry ingredients, ensuring they are evenly distributed.

Combine Wet Ingredients:
- In a separate bowl, whisk together the eggs, vanilla extract, and fresh lime juice.

Form Dough:
- Make a well in the center of the dry ingredients and pour the wet ingredients into it. Mix until a dough forms. If the dough is too sticky, you can add a little more flour.

Shape Dough:
- Turn the dough out onto a floured surface and divide it in half. Shape each half into a log about 12 inches long and 1 1/2 inches wide. Place the logs on the prepared baking sheet, leaving some space between them.

Bake First Round:
- Bake in the preheated oven for 25-30 minutes or until the logs are set and just starting to turn golden brown.

Cool and Slice:
- Allow the logs to cool for about 15 minutes, then use a sharp knife to slice them diagonally into 1/2-inch slices.

Bake Second Round:
- Arrange the slices cut side down on the baking sheet and bake for an additional 15-20 minutes or until the biscotti are golden brown and crisp.

Prepare Glaze:
- While the biscotti are cooling, prepare the glaze. Whisk together powdered sugar and fresh lime juice until smooth.

Glaze Biscotti:
- Once the biscotti have cooled completely, drizzle the glaze over the top. If desired, sprinkle chopped pistachios on top of the glaze.

Serve and Enjoy:
- Serve these delightful Lime and Pistachio Biscotti with your favorite hot beverage and enjoy the citrusy and nutty flavors!

Note:

- Storage: Store the biscotti in an airtight container at room temperature. They also freeze well for longer storage.
- Adjust Consistency: If the glaze is too thick, add a little more lime juice. If it's too thin, add more powdered sugar until you achieve the desired consistency.

These Lime and Pistachio Biscotti are twice-baked to achieve a crunchy texture, making them perfect for dipping into your favorite coffee or tea. The combination of zesty lime and nutty pistachios creates a unique and delicious flavor profile. Enjoy these biscotti as a sweet treat or thoughtful homemade gift!